You Matter

Dhiman

ISBN: 9798665988283

First published: July 2020

Cover design and image: Siobhan O'Dwyer @odwyer_sio9

You Matter

for someone in need of light

Dhiman

contents

d a w n

slowly but surely
in all the beautiful
and worthy ways
you are still blooming

i hope you always
have the courage
to love yourself
no matter
how many times
the world
breaks your heart

look deeply
into your heart
with kindness and love
and the key
of understanding
will reveal itself

all that you
need to let go
will lead you to
what is truly yours

you won't learn and grow
when it easy

you will learn and grow
when it's messy,
when it's most difficult

when we love ourselves as we are
while striving to be better everyday
aiming to live to our truest potential
we show appreciation
for the gifts we've been given
and honor the beauty of uniqueness
we carry in our heart

You Matter

all our feelings are necessary
even the ones that hurt us,

it is only when we acknowledge them
that we allow ourselves to be free
from the burden of carrying what hurts us

when everything
starts to settle down
and all that you have lost
make way for the things
you have prayed for
i hope you'll remember
what it took for you
to get to this place
the courage you needed
to give love to yourself

– *inner light*

they asked her,
"how do you make your heart stronger?"

she replied,
"love yourself before loving others."

– a strong heart

until i find the courage
to love myself
the world
will always feel like
a hurting place

– healing

You Matter

it still hurts her heart
to remember
all that she went through
but she is stronger now
and no longer afraid of the dark
for she knows that even here
she's valued and worthy of all the love

Dhiman

and if you ever have one of those days that you feel like you are not enough, that you'll never be whole again, just hold onto yourself with more kindness and love and remember – you are enough, you were enough and you'll always be enough, even on those days when you don't feel it that way.

– note to self | you are whole, you are enough

our true love for others
comes from loving ourselves first

how wonderful it is
to remember that
despite all these difficulties
there is still hope
to be found
in this life

be brave enough to love
but strong enough to let go

remember:
you can be afraid
and still have the courage
to do it anyway

— purpose

to truly understand and heal
the sufferings of others
first i must understand and heal
the sufferings of my own

– healing the self

and despite their own pain and suffering,
there are people in the world
who reach out to others
with their wounded hearts
and still dare to love

– heart of compassion

the most beautiful thing about life
is that no matter
what happened to you in the past
or where you stand
at this very moment,
you have the power
to heal your heart
and you can always start anew

before you go out into the world today, remember:

it's okay to be afraid. it's okay if you don't know who you are yet. we all have different timelines of discovering life, our own unique ways of figuring things out. maybe you still aren't sure if the path you are taking is right for you. it's okay, don't judge yourself for not knowing everything all at once. we all find our way through falling and rising, by taking chances. there are no shortcuts to live this life, and if we keep on waiting for the right time or the right way to truly start living it, we will be waiting here forever.

in all your difficulties
you are still blooming

"how do i get rid of my fear?"

"do what you would do if you were not afraid."

– courage

gentle reminder:

it will take time
it will hurt for a while
but in the end
it will be alright

– hope

when someone leaves you,
wish them happiness

but don't let your life slip away
waiting for them to come back,

wrap yourself in your own love
and move on,
you deserve better

– note to self | self-worth

to worry
is to give something else
the responsibility for your life

we are strongest in our most difficult

3 things you are in control of:

your response to your feelings
what you hold onto
what you let go

from the heartbreaks
that weighed her down
to the mountains she carried
to be where she is now
she has grown to be stronger
holding courage in her soul

it's okay to be unsure of who you are and what you are doing. the world might be telling you that you must have all the answers to find your meaning in this life, but know this: you don't have to know it all to find your value on this earth. you are here because you are needed, because you are loved. it's okay if you are slow in your progress, if you aren't growing the way others are. your life has its own timing, it has its own pace of growing. it doesn't have to match with others to be worthy, to be happy.

goal: take your own path, pace and time to grow. do not rush your progress or change yourself to end up becoming someone else. no one else in the world can do what you can do just by being you. your authenticity is your super power, the gateway to your happiness and fulfillment.

remember
the miles you have walked
just to be where you are now

even here in this chaos
you can still find
your reason to stay

life becomes less stressful
when you know who you are
and honor it
with self-acceptance and love

a well-nourished today
leads to a healthy
and well-prepared tomorrow

sunrise

i'm still learning to embrace life the way it is
despite the changes happening around me

that is the beauty of life –
just when you thought that
you have reached the end,
you somehow found a way
to begin again

if you ever find something that brings joy into your aching heart – embrace it, hold onto it with all you've got. there are many things that life may have taken away from you, and many of them you'll never get back. perhaps this, this little sparkle of light in your heart is life's way of paying back. sometimes, there are no answers to our suffering. but there is always hope, and for that you and i must look forward, even if there is darkness, even if there is pain in our heart.

goal: if you open your heart and mind to the endless possibilities that exist in the world, you will notice that there is still so much for you to look forward to, a new life waiting for you to discover.

one day you'll look back and find—
even when things did not go your way
or turn out to be right,
you were still moving ahead
with unshakable hope and courage
towards never ending light

You Matter

i hope you know
it's okay to be slow
to feel hopeless
in not knowing
which way to go
but even here
you are allowed to trust
to take courage
and believe that
even the darkest of paths
can lead you
to your greatest of life

keep going
some days it won't feel easy,
but you have to keep going
even in the uncertainty of things,
you have to move ahead with hope,
for the bad days will not stay
and you will find your way

even though she is hurt
she is not afraid to start again
for she knows that
even here in this darkness
the pain she is feeling
will not stay
and with her love and courage
she will get through this anyway

remember:
your feelings
only make you human,
they do not define who you are

when we appreciate and accept life in the way that it unfolds, we allow ourselves to let go of the idea of perfection; and as we learn to look at life in a non-judgmental way, we find beauty in the imperfect, we notice peace in the chaos, and as a result, we nourish our soul and the world in a harmonious and loving way.

goal: appreciate life. accept its unpredictability. perfection is only an illusion. imperfection is where true joy and peace lie.

and when the world hurts you,
breaks you, attempts to change you
remember to always come back to yourself,
to hold onto yourself and
everyday carry in your heart
some love
to give to your own self

part of loving yourself
is also not to judge yourself
when you feel different

– self-compassion

you are not a caged bird
if you don't feel loved and needed
where you are,
remember you are allowed to let go
and go where you truly belong;

you don't have to apologize
for choosing yourself,
nor do you have to ask
for permission
to set yourself free

– let go and be free

true healing comes from
understanding and trusting
your own inner power

things that changed
will never be the same again
but i hope you know
even here in the uncertain
there is still room for you to grow
to keep trusting your heart
to hold onto yourself more

– looking inward

You Matter

you may not get to choose or change
everything in your life

but you can choose yourself
and you can begin again

Dhiman

she is slowly learning
to believe that
in their own time
the right things
will come into her life

you can be a lot of things
but you cannot be everything
and that's okay

– words that liberate

"does it ever stop hurting?"

"no, it doesn't. but as you move forward, as you begin to trust life's plans for you, you will learn to embrace it and in it you will find your courage, your reason to keep going."

You Matter

and may be what keeps us going
through the darkest hours of our life,
is the very reason that the sun comes out
even after a stormy night

i hope you know
there is nothing wrong
in trying again
in hoping for things
to change
even if today
doesn't look that way

– note to a weary heart | keep going

love yourself
for everything that you
already are
for how much you have
grown
and how far you have
come

and when it hurts
the best thing you can do
is to walk through it all
is to feel it all the way
until it begins to turn into healing
until it no longer hurts the same way

ask yourself:

is this feeling worth holding on or is it something that is
not allowing me to grow?

(and then act according to what feels right for you)

the root cause of our unhappiness:

we overvalue others and what they say
but never enough to ourselves

no matter what happens,
who stays and who doesn't,
know that things will change
and you will grow,
like the darkest of the nights
you will always make it through

– new dawn

letting go
is the art of
holding onto yourself more

two ways to simplify life:

1. decide what's important
2. let go what isn't

nothing in the world
can heal your heart
if you don't love
and accept
who you are

– healing is an inside job

you are not out of time. you are where you are supposed to be. take your time. walk on your path. it doesn't have to be easy. you only have to move ahead, believe in what your heart knows and trust that you will learn to grow.

letting go of someone you love, hurts

but holding onto someone
who may never love you back, hurts more

when you have
peace in your mind
you bring
peace into the world

– inner peace

and on those days
when your progress doesn't seem
to make any sense, when your path
is laid down in darkness
and you don't have any clue
if there's light waiting for you
at the other end, remember–
there were times in your life
when you thought you wouldn't survive
but with courage and hope in your heart
you have made it through every single time

– you'll make it through

maybe
what lies ahead
is greater than
what you expected

– stay

wherever you are
no matter what you are
going through,
you are not alone
in feeling this,
you are not alone
in this mess of things

– we are together in this

remember,
sometimes growth will look like
staying still and taking your time
to heal

all these
l i t t l e s t e p s
will add up
i n t h e e n d

just because someone has treated you unkindly doesn't mean you are unworthy of kindness. just because someone has made you feel unloved doesn't mean you don't deserve love. remember, when someone says hurtful things to you or acts in a way that hurts your heart, they are only showing the hurt they are carrying within themselves. their action reflects who they are, not what you deserve.

goal: know your worth. do not let someone else's judgements and opinions dim the light in your heart.

"how do I heal what hurts me still?"

"be patient with your heart while the feeling is still new and do not judge it. remember – it's not there to harm you but to teach you a lesson that you must learn in order to help your heart grow. be open to how it makes you feel and do not run away from it or suppress it if you feel pain in your heart. be kind to yourself as you learn to let go of it and with time when you get through this, you'll begin to notice peace and comfort in your heart."

goal: treat your wounds with love. be kind to yourself on the days that it feels too hard to carry on. healing takes time. growth is a lifelong journey. selflove is a continuous process.

walk away, preserve your peace

not all that is broken needs to be fixed

it's okay
if all you did today
was make yourself happy

when you love yourself first
you show the world
what you truly deserve

new day

the goal
is not to become
what the world
wants you to be
but to be more
of who you are
and what you dream
of becoming

you will heal
and you will grow
when you allow yourself
to feel and learn to let go

and she smiled and said,

"no matter how difficult life turns out to be, i hope you'll never give up on its possibility to change."

perhaps
what you have been seeking
is not here yet
but even in this waiting
i hope you know
you still belong
and you still have
a place of your own

maybe you are uncertain about the future and you don't know which road to take or what to love. but even here you must not forget about your strength, the light that is shining in your heart. life might have its difficulties but you, my friend, are strong enough to rise through them. let life slowly unfold itself without worrying about what's next. trust that whatever it is that is best for you, will happen.

goal: patience and perseverance always pay off. when you focus too much on the achievements and forget to enjoy and appreciate the journey, you miss the beauty of the present moment, the joy that can be found only in the little things.

happiness is being okay
with who you are
without justifying
your worth to the world

You Matter

no matter what season of growth
you go through,
may you always have the strength
to hang in there,
to trust in the good
that is meant for you

Dhiman

remember, a smile doesn't always mean you are happy. sometimes it means that even though what you are going through might be difficult, you are still strong enough to face it.

You Matter

sometimes
the bravest thing you can do for yourself
is to walk away from things
that no longer belong to you
knowing that you will not miss
anything that is truly meant for you

and one day she realized
she no longer had to hold onto
the feelings that hurt her heart,
she can simply allow herself
to feel them and then when she is ready,
she can gently let them go and set herself free

to the people you belong
you'll always be enough
and never too much

it's okay if you are yet to know what to do in life. sometimes the answers you seek do not arrive the way you anticipate. sometimes they come in the disguise of pain, heartbreaks and setbacks. keep your heart open and trust that even if you can't see the way out right now, it is there and if you keep on moving with faith, you will find your way through it.

goal: trust life's plans for your life when you feel uncertain, when you feel afraid of what's ahead. remember, there is always a way.

let it be slow and gentle,
forgiving someone takes time

it's okay
if today looks different
than what you had planned

you don't have to have all the answers to find your meaning in this world. you can take everything in your life as slowly and as gently as you want to and still have peace, still attain growth. remember that life doesn't expect you to know it all. all that it wants you to do is to be yourself, to grow in your own way without judging yourself, without putting yourself to any kind of comparison with another human being. for life brought you here to be you, simply, unapologetically you.

goal: you are enough the way you are. your uniqueness is what lights up the world. never let anyone or anything make you doubt your worth.

there was a time in your life
when you were afraid of the dark
for you couldn't see the light
or hope on your path
but somehow someway
you have made it through
to get to this place
where you are free to be you

she may not know
what the future holds
but she is still here,
trusting her heart
holding onto hope

some people spend their whole life waiting for the right time, the right opportunity to come their way. they let their circumstances, their difficulties, decide what kind of life they get to live. never do they dare to make their own way nor do they allow themselves to follow what their heart says, until one day they find themselves standing at the edge of life, a life that was theirs yet they never had the courage to live it. do not let yourself be one of them.

goal: follow your heart, listen to your intuition. this is your one and only life. believe in miracles. believe in yourself too. take responsibility for your life. do what you think is best for you.

what you feel about yourself, matters. how much you love and embrace your heart goes a long way in creating the strongest version of you. so, treat yourself kindly; encourage yourself when it's difficult. the road to self-growth and self-love is never easy. but when you are in love with the journey of your becoming, every obstacle you face along the way becomes a part of your growth and your healing.

goal: how you feel about yourself dictates the way you feel about the world. love yourself through every phase of your life's journey. this is the secret of true happiness. this is the way of finding joy in the midst of the uncertain.

slowly gently
all of this
will start
to make sense

– patience

what great joy it is
to be kind
to take a step back
and remember:
a person doesn't
have to perfect
in order to be
worthy of love

lesson for life:

you cannot escape the difficult days,
you can only learn to live through them

note:
even in the despair
make room for hope
for there is, always,
always hope

and even here
despite the unknowns
she is learning to trust her heart
she is choosing to grow

i hope you will choose yourself. even in the midst of all your doubts i hope you will remember that you still belong. i hope you will know that nothing in the world can take away your worth, no matter what you achieve or what you don't. it's okay if you need to slow down. it's okay if you need to change your path. just keep on trusting your heart even when going gets tough, for there is hope beyond the hard days and there is light waiting for you at the other end.

goal: choose yourself every single day, over and over again.

even in the shadows
of the unknown,
in waiting for a new dawn,
know that you are needed
and even here, you still belong

gentle reminder:

you don't have to wait for things to change
in order to begin again

3 things to do for yourself today:

be more kind to yourself
find joy in the process
be gentle with your progress

You Matter

may you never forget
that even though it was difficult,
you didn't give up on yourself;
you hung in there till the end
and with unprecedented courage
you have made your way through the darkness

you don't have to wait for your circumstances to change to believe in the goodness of life. you can trust in the goodness of life no matter where you stand at this very moment. maybe things have been difficult lately and you are uncertain about everything. but even here in this hopelessness, you can trust in the value of your life and know that you are here because you are worthy, because you belong. your difficulties and circumstances do not define your worth. the love and courage in your heart define your worth. you, my friend, define your worth.

goal: remind yourself of the things that will truly matter in the end: love, hope, joy, kindness and all the light that you carry in your heart.

there will be many things in life that you won't have control over. they will cripple you, hurt you, break you into pieces but they will also build your character, change you completely as a person. so, when you encounter them, don't fear them. welcome them as opportunities to grow, to be a better version of you. you will be hurt but in the same process you will learn how to find a stronger you.

goal: every hardship that you encounter opens up unique opportunities for you to grow. embrace the hard times as growth times, instead of running away from them.

once you loosen the grip
on the thought that you need
acceptance from others
in order to know that your life matters,
you begin to see yourself as someone
already worthy, loved and valued,
just the way you are

never forget
the ones
who loved you
even when you
couldn't love yourself

sometimes
it's the little changes
that changes everything

being grateful doesn't mean you have to love every part of your life. it's okay to feel hurt when something doesn't turn out the way you thought it to be, especially for things you have given so much of your heart. what gratefulness means is that no matter what happens or what you go through, you are able to appreciate the journey, the greater purpose of those struggling moments and have faith in your heart that you are already enough and what you deserve will find its way in the right time.

goal: think about all the things and people you still have in your life. ask yourself: how can i be more grateful today?

it's not your fault if someone doesn't stay. sometimes life has different plans for us, sometimes people have their own reasons to walk away. it's not that you are unworthy of being loved, it only means that you deserve someone else, someone worthy of your heart. sometimes, life makes us wait so that it can prepare us for the better things. always trust that life has its plans for us. even if it doesn't turn out the way we think, it always works out for our good in the end.

goal: understand that sometimes you won't have the answer to certain problems in life. liberate your heart from trying to control what can't be controlled.

You Matter

there is someone out in the world
who loves you as wildly as you are

healing
=
discomfort > acceptance > growth

everything that i have been through
gave me the strength to be
who i am today

– growth

it's okay to be slow
we all grow differently

You Matter

even here
in the days of your difficulties
do not forget to remind yourself:
i'm still worthy of love
i'm still worthy of being free

take time for yourself. life is happening here and now. there is no need to hurt your heart with people's expectations and judgements. let go. find what sets you free and then hold onto it. life is already beautiful; you are already enough.

You Matter

Dhiman

Made in the USA
Coppell, TX
01 April 2021